EXTRAORDINARY ANIMALS

ARMORED ANIMALS

Andrew Brown

CRABTREE
Publishing Company

CRABTREE
Publishing Company

350 Fifth Avenue	360 York Road, R.R.4	73 Lime Walk
Suite 3308	Niagara-on-the-Lake	Headington, Oxford
New York, NY 10118	Ontario L0S 1J0	England OX3 7AD

Editor **Bobbie Kalman**
Assistant Editor **Petrina Gentile**
Designer **Melissa Stokes**

Illustrations by

Front cover: Matthew Hillier/WLAA (main), Rachel Lockwood/WLAA, Valérie Stetten; Back cover: Robin Boutell/WLAA
Robin Boutell/WLAA (p. 6–7), Robin Budden/WLAA (p. 18–19, 28–29), Barry Croucher/WLAA (p. 20–21, 31),
Tony Hargreaves (p. 21), Matthew Hillier/WLAA (p. 22–25), Rachel Lockwood/WLAA (p. 8–9, 16–17, 27),
William Oliver/WLAA (p. 30–31), Valérie Stetten (p. 12–15), Kim Thompson (p. 10–11)

Created by
Marshall Cavendish Books
(a division of Marshall Cavendish Partworks Ltd.)
119 Wardour Street, London, W1V 3TD, England

First printed 1997
Copyright © 1997 Marshall Cavendish Ltd.

Cataloging-in-Publication Data

Brown, Andrew, 1972-
Armored animals
(Extraordinary animals series)
Includes index.
ISBN 0-86505-558-0 (bound)   ISBN 0-86505-566-1 (pbk.)
1. Body covering (Anatomy) – Juvenile literature.
2. Animal defenses – Juvenile literature.
I. Title.   II. Series: Brown, Andrew, 1972-   .   Extraordinary animals series.
QL942.B76 1997   j591.1'858   LC 96-46983

Printed and bound in Malaysia

CONTENTS

INTRODUCTION

The world can be a very dangerous place for some creatures. Hungry hunting animals, called predators, are always searching for something tasty to eat. Many animals have special ways to protect themselves against predators. Some animals have thick, tough skin, and others are covered with shells or layers of bone. Many also have spines or horns to fight attackers—or even each other!

LARGE HORNS help bighorn sheep, below, fight. They fight each other to see who is the strongest in the group.

SHARP SPINES

cover the bodies of some animals. They protect the hedgehog from most predators.

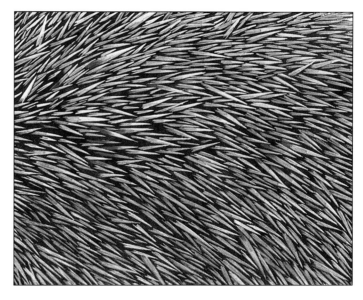

THICK SKINS

protect animals, such as the armadillo and the rhinoceros from the bites of lions and other hunters.

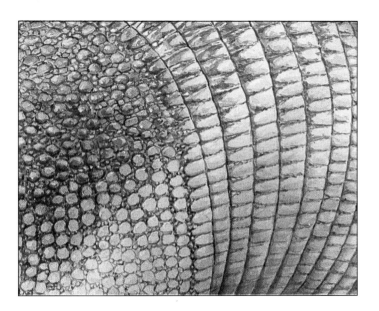

HARD SHELLS

are very difficult to break open. They cover the soft bodies of animals such as turtles.

ARMADILLOS

Armadillos live in the grasslands of North and South America. Their name comes from the Spanish word *armado*, which means "armored one." The armadillo's tough skin makes this animal look as if it is wearing a suit of armor.

Hard, bony plates cover the armadillo's body. The plates are arranged in bands over its back. The bands are attached to soft skin. The hard plates protect the armadillo against enemies and insect bites.

THE EYES ▶▶▶
have thick lids to protect them from insect bites.

THE SNOUT ▶▶▶
is long and pointed. The armadillo uses its strong sense of smell to find insects up to 8 inches (20 cm) below the ground!

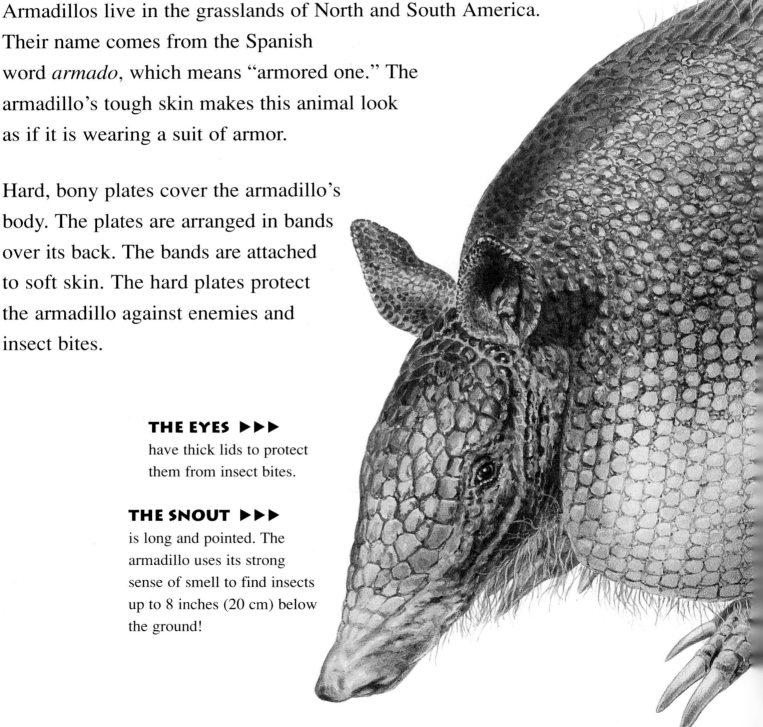

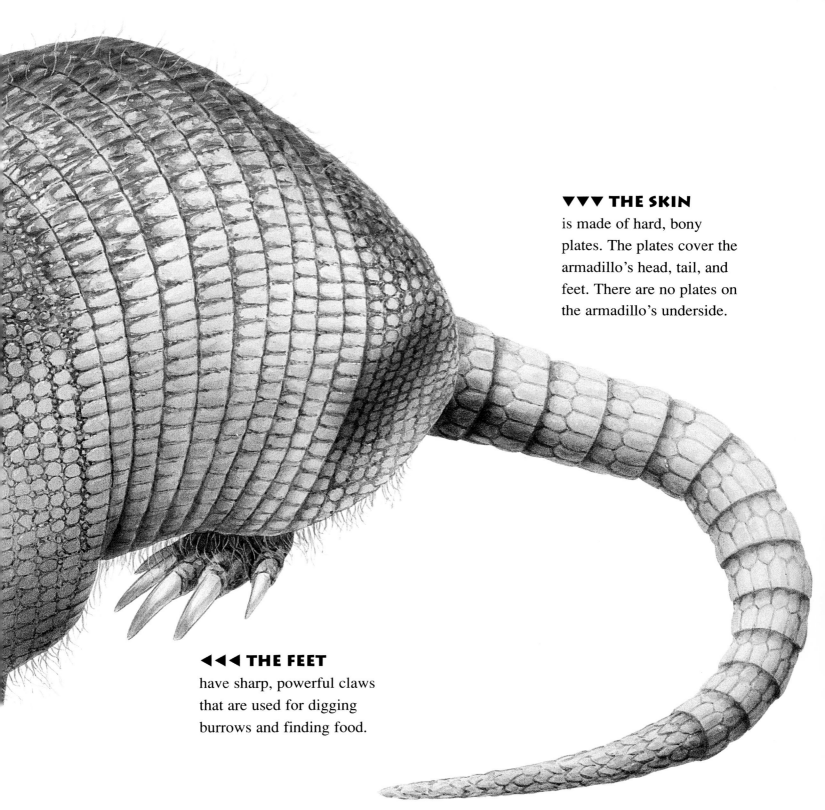

▼▼▼ THE SKIN

is made of hard, bony plates. The plates cover the armadillo's head, tail, and feet. There are no plates on the armadillo's underside.

◄◄◄ THE FEET

have sharp, powerful claws that are used for digging burrows and finding food.

Most armadillos live in deep underground burrows. They dig the burrows very quickly. Their strong front legs loosen the dirt, and their back legs kick it out of the way.

Armadillos spend most of the day sleeping in burrows. At night, the armadillo leaves its burrow to look for ants, termites, and small animals. It digs straight into the middle of anthills and termite mounds. The armadillo's armor protects it from thousands of insect bites. Using its long, sticky tongue, an armadillo can eat as many as 40,000 ants in a single meal!

Armadillos are powerful diggers. They dig to search for food and escape from danger. Although armadillos are covered with armor, they run or burrow when they are frightened by enemies.

ROLLING DEFENSES

When in danger, the three-banded armadillo rolls itself into a tight ball. Its head, tail, and armor fit together so well that enemies can find no gaps to break through.

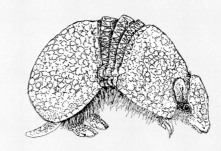

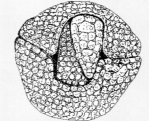 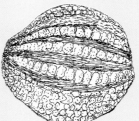

KEEP OUT!

A giant armadillo protects its burrow from a tayra, a weasel-like animal from South America.

PANGOLINS

The pangolin lives in the tropical parts of Africa and Asia. Its long body is covered with overlapping, brown scales.

Pangolins are timid and live alone or in pairs. When it senses danger, the pangolin curls into a ball. Its sharp scales also stand up. Most animals, except for big cats and hyenas, cannot break through the pangolin's shield.

Pangolins use their strong sense of smell to find food. They eat termites, ants, and other insects.

Humans are the pangolin's greatest enemy. The pangolin's meat is very popular with some African tribes. Its scales are made into jewelry. Sometimes the scales are also used to make medicine.

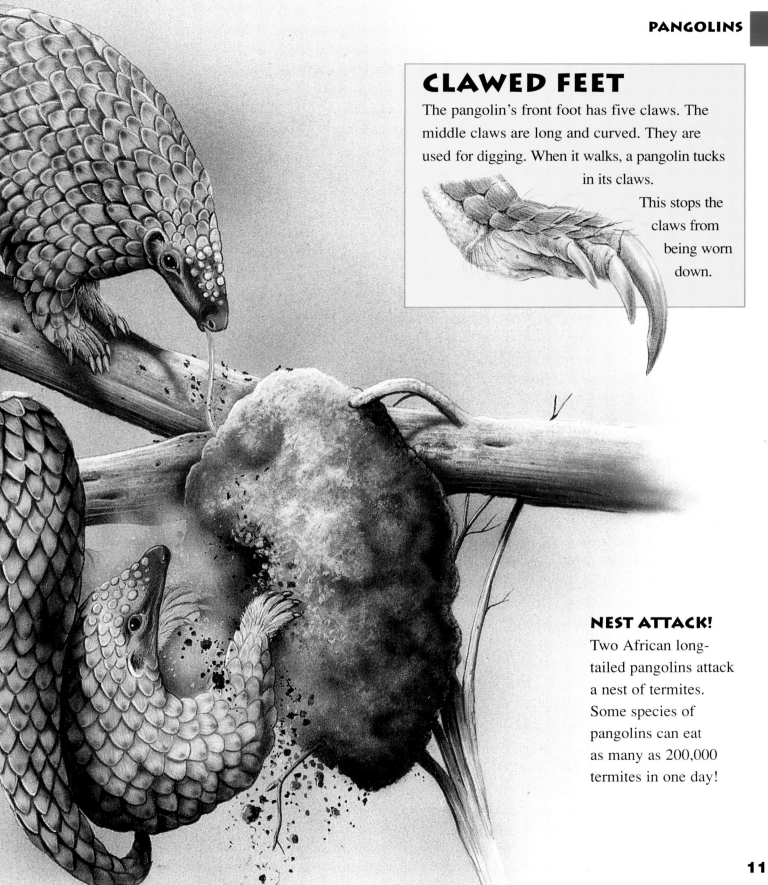

CLAWED FEET

The pangolin's front foot has five claws. The middle claws are long and curved. They are used for digging. When it walks, a pangolin tucks in its claws.

This stops the claws from being worn down.

NEST ATTACK!

Two African long-tailed pangolins attack a nest of termites. Some species of pangolins can eat as many as 200,000 termites in one day!

TURTLES

Turtles are reptiles. Many reptiles have body armor. The turtle has a tough shell—it is one of the strongest armors in the animal kingdom.

Turtles that live on land have thick, heavy shells to protect them against animal bites. Only hyenas and crocodiles can bite through a turtle's shell.

Turtles that live in the sea have lighter, flatter shells than land turtles. The shape of their shells helps them move easily in the water. The light weight allows them to float.

Some people hunt turtles. They use the shells of turtles to make combs, frames for eyeglasses, and pens.

▲▲▲
THE EYES
are the turtle's main way of finding food, such as soft plants and small animals. Turtles have excellent vision. They can see colors and shapes—even in dark water.

▼▼▼ THE SHELL

is covered in scales. The number of rings on the scales shows the age of the turtle.

THE TURTLE'S X-RAY

carapace

plastron

The turtle's shell has two main pieces—the carapace on the back and the plastron underneath. The shell has an outer layer of scales, called scutes, and an inner layer of bony plates. The skeleton is partly attached to the carapace.

◄◄◄ THE FINGERS

are joined together to make flippers. The front flippers are much longer than the back ones. When swimming, the flippers propel the turtle through water.

CROCODILES

Crocodiles are reptiles. They live in the rivers of Africa, Asia, Australia, and North and South America.

Like all reptiles, crocodiles have scaly, waterproof skin. A bony shield covers the skin on the crocodile's back.

Crocodiles are cold-blooded animals. They have no way of keeping their bodies warm. Crocodiles need sunshine to keep warm. To build up strength before they attack their prey, crocodiles must come out of the water and warm themselves in the sun.

▼▼▼ **THE EYES**

are on top of the crocodile's head. This helps the crocodile see above water when it is swimming. A third eyelid protects the eyes when diving.

▲▲▲ **THE TEETH**

are cone shaped. They are designed for holding prey, not for chewing or cutting.

The crocodile uses its strong jaws and teeth to catch an animal and drag it beneath the water until it drowns. It stores the body underwater until it rots. The crocodile will come back later to eat its prey.

SCALY CREATURES

Crocodiles are covered with thousands of tiny scales. The scales are made of dead tissue called keratin, the same material as is found in human 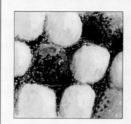 fingernails. Crocodiles continually lose their old scales and grow new ones. Sometimes they can lose all their skin at once!

▲▲▲ THE STOMACH

contains strong juices and pebbles, which help the crocodile digest its food. The crocodile eats all its prey, including bones, hooves, and horns.

▲▲▲ THE TAIL

is very long, muscular, and flat. The crocodile uses its tail to push itself forward when it swims.

PORCUPINES

Porcupines are slow-moving animals that have an amazing defense—thousands of needle-sharp spines called quills.

The North American porcupine, which lives across Canada and the United States, has more than 30,000 quills on its body! Each quill is covered with tiny spikes. Few predators dare to attack the porcupine.

THE HEAD ▶▶▶
is small. Although the porcupine has very poor eyesight, it has excellent hearing.

THE FEET ▶▶▶
are broad and heavy. The soles have small, hard pads and long, sharp claws to help the porcupine climb trees.

◀◀◀ THE QUILLS
are hollow and covered with thousands of tiny spikes. When in danger, the porcupine's quills stand on end.

A BIG DIFFERENCE!
The North American porcupine, center, can grow up to 4 ft (120 cm). The African species, left, looks bigger because of its long quills, but it is not. It can grow up to 3 ft (85 cm). The long-tailed species of Asia, right, is the smallest—it grows up to 1.5 ft (48 cm).

If a porcupine stabs an enemy with one of its quills, the quill snaps off and stays in the animal's flesh. If a predator, such as a lion, gets a quill stuck in its throat, it may starve to death. Porcupine quills do not always kill their victims. Animals have been known to survive for years with quills stuck in their bodies.

The porcupine's deadliest enemy is the fisher, a weasel-like animal. The fisher flips the porcupine onto its back and attacks the porcupine's unprotected stomach. It may take the fisher 30 minutes to kill a porcupine, but it gives the fisher enough food to last two weeks.

NOISE MAKERS

The African porcupine has a bunch of short, cup-shaped quills at the tip of its tail. The quills rattle when the porcupine shakes its tail. This noise helps keep away enemies.

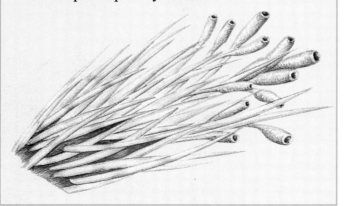

A LION

cannot hurt a porcupine. If
it tries to attack a porcupine,
the lion may get a quill stuck
in its throat or mouth.

HEDGEHOGS

Hedgehogs may seem cute and cuddly, but they are not! If you picked one up, you would be pricked by one of its long, sharp spines. The spines cover the hedgehog's back and protect it from enemies and insect bites.

The spines are white and brown. They are made of lots of hairs, which are packed closely together. They protect the hedgehog from enemies such as foxes. If it sees a fox, the hedgehog curls up into a ball to hide its soft stomach.

Each spine is hollow and has a narrow part called the neck. If the animal falls, or is hit by something, the neck bends and softens the blow to its body.

THE LONG NOSE ▶▶▶
is always damp, which helps the hedgehog find prey. The hedgehog has an excellent sense of smell.

THE LEGS ▶▶▶
are very long for such a small animal. The feet have five powerful claws for digging.

▼▼▼ THE SPINES

are about one inch
(25 mm) long and cover
the hedgehog's back. Some
hedgehogs have as many
as 7,000 spines!

YOUNG DEFENDERS

When hedgehog babies
are about 11 days
old, they practice
curling up into
a ball.

RHINOS

The rhinoceros looks like a fierce dinosaur, but it is not. It is a gentle animal that would rather run from trouble than face it.

The word rhinoceros means "nose horn." Rhinos are the only animals with horns on their nose. Like human fingernails, the rhino's horns are made of keratin. Some species of rhinos, such as the white rhino, can grow horns up to five feet (150 cm) long!

THE HORNS ▶▶▶
are strong and sharp. They are attached to a large lump on the rhino's nose.

RHINO LIPS ▶▶▶
are big and pointed. Their shape helps it hold on to tall grasses and leaves.

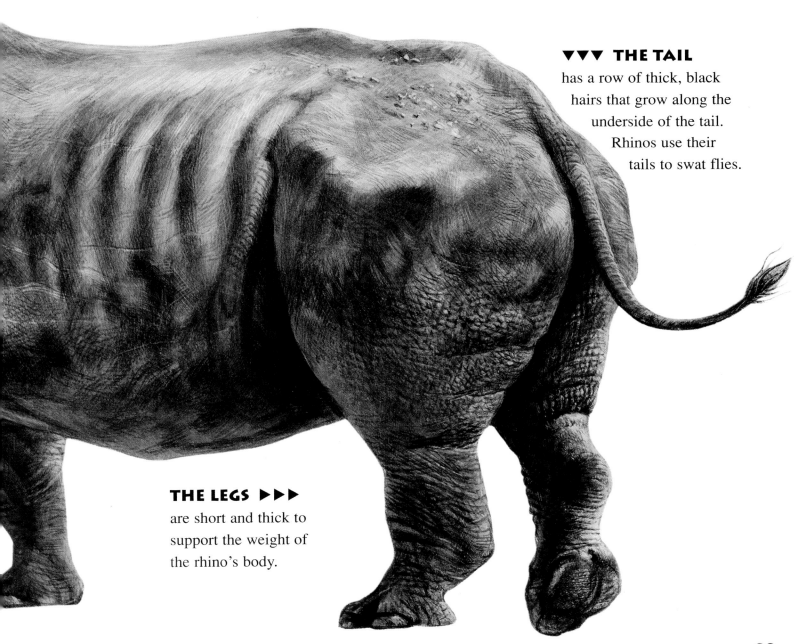

▼▼▼ THE HUMP

on the back of the rhino's
neck helps support the
animal's head.

▼▼▼ THE TAIL

has a row of thick, black
hairs that grow along the
underside of the tail.
Rhinos use their
tails to swat flies.

THE LEGS ▶▶▶

are short and thick to
support the weight of
the rhino's body.

As well as its horns, the rhino's large size and thick skin
protect it from enemies. The Indian rhino's skin is very thick
and hangs in folds. It even has a special fold to protect its tail.

The rhino has few predators. Lions and hyenas kill
baby rhinos, but humans are the most serious
threat. Humans often kill rhinos for their
horns. Some people use the horns to
make medicine or horn-handled
knives. Some species of
rhinos, such as the black
rhino, are almost extinct.

DANGER
brings rhinos together.
They stand with their
tails together
and their heads
outward, so enemies
cannot hurt them.

THICK-SKINNED

All rhinos have bumpy, hairless skin. The skin of the Javan rhino looks scaly and has a mosaic pattern all over it. The Indian rhino's skin is unevenly patterned. Its shoulder and upper leg areas are covered with wartlike bumps. The rest of its body is smooth.

JAVAN RHINO

INDIAN RHINO

GOAT ANTELOPES

There are many kinds of goat antelopes around the world. They include domestic sheep and goats, ibex, and bighorns. Most goat antelopes have horns.

Some goat antelopes live on their own. Sometimes they are attacked by groups of large animals. They use their horns to protect themselves against fierce attackers, such as bears.

Other kinds of goat antelopes live in large groups, called herds. They look after each other if one is attacked. The horns of these antelopes are very large.

The ibex on page 27 has long, curved horns. The male ibex uses its horns to attract females and show off its strength by fighting other males in the herd. The fights show which animal is the strongest.

◄◄◄ THE HORNS

grow from the animal's forehead. Some goat antelopes have short, sharp horns. Others, such as the ibex below, have long, curved horns.

▼▼▼ THE IBEX

molts its coat every year in the spring. During the fall and winter, the coat grows thicker to keep the animal warm.

▲▲▲ THE BEARD

of the ibex, above, is short. Some goat antelopes have very long beards.

THE LEGS ►►►

are sturdy and strong. The hooves have sharp edges to grip rocky cliffs.

Bighorn sheep are another kind of goat antelope. They have huge, curved horns. Male bighorns often run and crash their heads together. These noisy fights can last for hours.

The bighorns are usually not hurt. They have very strong head and neck bones that protect them. Sometimes, however, one of the animals may be killed.

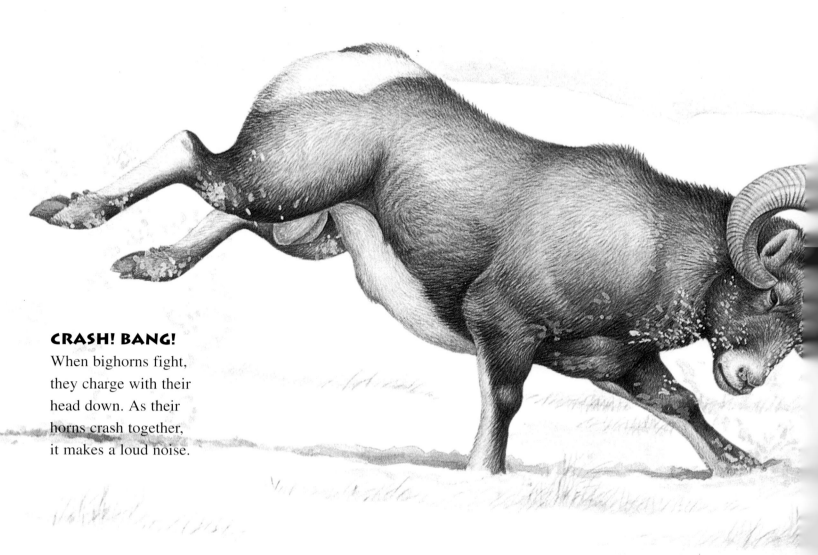

CRASH! BANG!
When bighorns fight, they charge with their head down. As their horns crash together, it makes a loud noise.

KINDS OF HORNS

There are many different kinds of horns in the goat antelope family. Markhors have large, corkscrew horns. Saigas have short, sharp horns for piercing attackers. Male bighorns use their curved horns to fight for mates.

MARKHOR   **SAIGA**   **BIGHORN**

DEER

Most male deer grow antlers. The antlers are made of bone and grow from bumps on the deer's head. Some deer have antlers with simple spikes. Others, such as the red deer on the right, have antlers that look like branches. Each April, the male deer loses its antlers and grows a new pair. When they are growing, the antlers are covered with tiny, protective hairs, called velvet. After a few months, the velvet hardens. The deer rubs its antlers against trees to remove the velvet.

Deer use their antlers to fight each other. They can get badly hurt. Sometimes two deer can even get their antlers stuck together during a fight!

▲▲▲ THE EYES

are large and set high on the head. They are very sensitive to movements, so the deer can spot a stalking predator. The deer can see almost in a circle.

THE HOOVES ▼▼▼

are slightly curved, which helps the deer have a strong grip when it runs.

◀◀◀ THE ANTLERS

grow larger as the deer gets older. Males use them to fight and win their position in the social group.

THE MOOSE

The moose is the largest deer. Moose live in Canada and the United States. They also live in Europe and Asia, where they are known as elk.

◀◀◀ THE RUMP

often has a white patch. To signal danger, the deer lifts its tail. The other deer see the white patch and run away.

INDEX

GLOSSARY

antler – one of the branched horns that grow on the head of male deer and other related animals

burrow – a hole dug in the ground by an animal for living or hiding

cold-blooded – describes an animal whose body temperature changes with the weather

defense – a way of protecting against attack, injury, or danger

extinct – something that no longer exists

hyena – an animal with powerful jaws that lives in Africa and Asia and resembles a wolf

keratin – a hard substance found in horns, hoofs, hair, and nails

molt – to shed an outer layer, such as skin or feathers, and grow a new one

plates – a thin, flat layer of scale or skin found on armadillos and related animals

predator – an animal that hunts and kills other animals for food

prey – an animal that is hunted by another animal for food

quill – one of the sharp spines of a porcupine or hedgehog

skeleton – the framework of bones that protects and supports the body of an animal with a backbone

waterproof – something that will not let water pass through